"Anyone

Weld

A Step-By-Step Guide on the Fundamentals of Welding

Written and Illustrated by:

R.T. George, Jr.

TABLE OF CONTENTS

INTRODUCTION

"I don't care if what you weld gets buried fifty feet underground, you make the best weld possible because one day someone will see it."

This was told to me on my first day working as a welder by a man, who at the time, had been welding for fifteen years. As I stood there looking lost and confused with my mouth wide open, I remember thinking how this man did not know me from Adam and yet he lays something like this on me. I had no idea of what he was trying to say. My friend must have been reading my mind because before I could reply he continued.

"What I mean is that you must take pride in your welding with every job you do. Without the pride and determination to do your best, that weld could break and, as a result, hurt or kill someone. If you can not do this get out of welding now."

I have never forgotten that conversation. Only through the years of working as a certified welder did I learn to understand and appreciate the meaning of my friend's words. I have seen welds break either because the welder broke procedure or did a halfway job just to get "through". Fortunately, very few people have been hurt and those who were, were not hurt seriously. This does not mean that my friend exaggerated. I have read many accident reports on welding where welders had been seriously injured and, one in particular, killed.

I hope that by now I have you shaking in your boots. Why? Without being aware of the possible risks and dangers involved in welding, not knowing the correct procedures and why they are important, and not having the willingness to learn each day, you will not make it as a welder. Anyone can weld but only those who are aware of the above factors and make them a part of their welding career will be good welders.

This welding manual will be different from any you will come across. If you really want to learn how to weld then I can teach you the art. It is up to you as to what you want to learn, what you do with what you learn, and how far you go with welding as a career.

I have covered the basic fundamentals of welding and left out a lot of the technical aspects of welding for I feel they are unimportant for the beginner. As a beginner it is important to learn what welding is and how to do it. Do not misinterpret my meaning. Technical data is important and there are several good books about welding that contain this information. I believe that it is easier to learn the fundamentals of welding without getting lost and confused by a lot of figures and bombarded with a host of graphs. Some diagrams are necessary and I have provided just enough to help you understand what I am trying to teach.

If at any time you come across a welding term and do not know its meaning, turn to the "GLOSSARY OF WELDING TERMS" located at the end of this instructional manual. These terms are the ones most commonly used and heard in relation to welding. The glossary will come in handy until you become familiar with them though use as a welder.

Now it is time to learn how to weld. Please take the time necessary to read each section carefully. I have written this manual in such a way that each section will gradually increase you knowledge and skills in welding. As with learning anything new, "PRACTICE" is the key word. With practice comes dedication and those two in combination will make you a good welder.

SAFETY

We all have had lectures on safety. Usually we get bored and have a tendency to let most of what we hear go in one ear and out the other. Many people think that nothing will happen to them because they are careful and have enough common sense to avoid accidents. I was a guilty as the next person when it came to this way of thinking. It did not take long for me to realize that it was easier to learn from an experienced welder that it was from experience itself.

Please take this section seriously and never stop being safety conscious.

Accidents do happen and sometimes this is nothing you can do to prevent them from happening. However, you can prevent the majority of accidents by being aware and observant of your surroundings and of the people around you. This may involve you having to tell someone that he or she is not performing in a safe manner. It may also involve your refusal to perform a certain job assigned to you. Take notice that there is a difference between being safety conscious and being insubordinate. If you honestly feel that the conditions are not favorable to allow you to perform the assigned job safely then by all means refuse to do the job and state your reason or reasons why. Tempers may flair but they are a lot easier to deal with than an injury or possible death. A company that practices good safety standards will not fire you for your refusal to perform an assign task but rather work with you to correct the problem that will enable you to perform the work in a safe manner.

Cigarette smoking is dangerous to your health. Over a long period of time it could possibly kill you. We all know this and have been reminded of it so much that we can recite the warning label on cigarette packages from memory.

Where cigarettes take years, the smoke given off during welding will kill you in a matter of minutes because this smoke consumes oxygen.

When welding in a room or in closed quarters, never start welding without some source of ventilation. This may be accomplished by opening a window, a door, or by using a **Blower Unit** that sucks out the smoke. A blower unit works like a vacuum cleaner. A large accordion hose is connected to this unit and when the unit is turned on it inhales large amounts of welding smoke and discharges it somewhere else usually outdoors. Firefighters use this same equipment to reduce the amount of smoke in a given space.

Always wear protective clothing when welding such as long-sleeved shirts, long pants. welding gloves, and to be extra safe, leather welders sleeves and / or leather welders jacket. Welding produces a bright light that will burn your skin just like over exposure to sunlight produces a sunburn. In welding this is referred to as a *Flashburn.*

Welding rods while in use throw off a great deal of sparks that can burn your skin like a match when they come into contact with your skin. In addition, these same sparks can catch your clothing on fire.

I strongly recommend that you never wear synthetic materials while welding because if they should ever catch on fire they melt onto your skin rather than burn away.

Denim is by far the best material to wear while welding.

Leave your tennis shoes at home! When working around steel wear high-top boots, preferably steel-toed boots. That extra protection is a nice thing to have. All you have to do is drop a piece of steel on your foot one time to fully appreciate and understand the purpose of steel-toed boots.

The major complaint many people have about wearing steel-toed boots is that they make their feet cold all the time because the steel retains the cold. The question here is which is more desirable - warmer feet or safer feet? Only you can make that decision.

I am amazed when I see someone fresh out of welding school, or the so-called "professional", who is cocky and think they know all about welding. This is the type of person you see welding without the use of a welding shield (also known as a welding helmet). This usually occurs during *Tack Welding* (applying just enough weld to an area to hold something in place). Just as the light produced while welding can burn your skin, the same holds true for your eyes. A burn to your eyes due to this bright light is also known as a *flashburn.* A flash burn to your eyes will cause small blisters to form on your eyeball. When these blisters burst it really is uncomfortable. Your eyes will have a burning sensation and feel as though you have sand in your eyes.

No matter how careful you are your eyes will get *flashed* from time to time. Your alertness will determine as to what extent. A home remedy for minor flashburns to the eyes is to stay in a darkened room for eight to ten hours. This will allow your eyes to heal themselves. For added comfort cover your eyes with a dampened washcloth. Consult your physician for serious burns. Under no circumstances take chances with your eyes. They come first.

Always protect your eyes the best way possible by wearing your welding shield during welding.

The one type of flash I dislike most is getting *flashed* by another welder. At times this cannot be avoided because the welder did not know you were in the vicinity. When it does happen because the welder is inconsiderate by not really caring who is around him really makes me angry. Before starting to weld take the time to look all around you to make sure others nearby are safe. If they are within hearing distance caution them. The common phrase is ***Watch Your Eyes!*** This warning gives them time to avert their eyes. Use it!

One last point, if you are not sure of what you are doing then ask someone for assistance. Do not be like those who think they will figure it out, say to themselves that they are pretty sure of how to do it, or even think "that's good enough". You are taking a risk that someone, or yourself, could get hurt. If you ever get to the point where you think you know all you need to know about welding then that is the time to choose another career. From experience I know this way of thinking could cause serious injury to yourself or someone else. I have seen just that.

I cannot emphasize safety enough. Welding is a dangerous trade and this is why you have to be extra careful. Watch out for yourself and the people around you. Welding can be a fun and rewarding career but not at the expense of someone getting hurt.

BE SAFE

EQUIPMENT

You cannot learn how to weld without first becoming familiar with the equipment and accessories that are necessary for welding. There are four basic items you must have in order to weld:

(A) A Welding Machine
(B) An Electrode (welding rod)
(C) An Electrode Holder (stinger)
(D) A Welding Shield

All the knowledge in the world about welding is useless without the ability to use these four items proficiently. This is achieved only through repetitive use of the equipment. This chapter will explain what each item is and its function.

A Welding Machine

There are many different models of brand name welding machines on the market. When purchasing a welding machine always evaluate your welding needs and go from there. There is no need to buy an expensive model that will do everything but write your name. On the other hand, you will regret buying one that is too small and inefficient to handle your needs for welding. Ask questions about what a particular welding machine can or cannot do. Tell the salesperson what you plan to accomplish with this welding machine because he or she can be very helpful in you being able to select the proper welding machine for your needs. The bottom line is to know what you are buying before you buy it and, by the way, shop around for the best bargain.

No matter the brand or model of welding machine you purchase, they all work the same way. They all have a power output and some type of mechanism to regulate and adjust the amount of power (current) the machine produces. All welding machines have two electric terminals, referred to as *poles,* that are labeled *"Positive"* and *"Negative"*. The labeling for each terminal may be displayed as follows:

"Positive", *"+ "*, or *"Electrode"*   /   *"Negative"*, *" - "*, or *"To Work"*

No matter how it is displayed, positive is always positive and negative is always negative.

Positive and negative are very important because they determine the *Welding Polarity*. Welding polarity is described as the direction the electric current is moving as it passes through the object being welded. This electrical path begins at the negative terminal and ends at the positive terminal. The welder determines what polarity is needed before beginning to weld based on the type of welding electrode (welding rod) being used and the type of material to be welded. He accomplishes this by connecting the electrode holder (stinger) to either the positive or negative terminal on the welding machine.

There are two primary types of polarity used in welding. They are *Reversed Polarity* and *Straight Polarity.* The following will explain each type of polarity.

REVERSE POLARITY : The *electrode holder* is connected to the positive terminal on the welding machine and the *Ground* (negative cable) is connected to the negative terminal on the welding machine.

In this manner the electric current passes from the *ground* (negative cable), through the object being welded, and returns to the welding machine through the *electrode holder* (stinger). All electric currents *MUST* be grounded in order for the circuit to be complete or closed. In welding the object being welded is considered the ground and will always have the negative cable connected to it.

STRAIGHT POLARITY : The *electrode holder* is connected to the negative terminal on the welding machine and the *ground* (negative cable) is connected to the positive terminal on the welding machine.

In this manner the electric current passes from the ***electrode holder,*** through the object being welded, and returns to the welding machine through the ***ground*** (negative cable).

Instead of having to connect and disconnect the welding cables to determine polarity, some welding machines have a switch that you flip to determine polarity. On machines so equipped the electrode holder is always connected to the positive terminal on the welding machine and the ground (negative cable) is always connected to the negative terminal on the welding machine. This switch is considered a luxury item just as having cruise control on your car. The nice thing about this switch is that it eliminates the need to manually trace the welding cables back to the welding machine to see which cable is connected to which electric terminal.

(Fig 1)

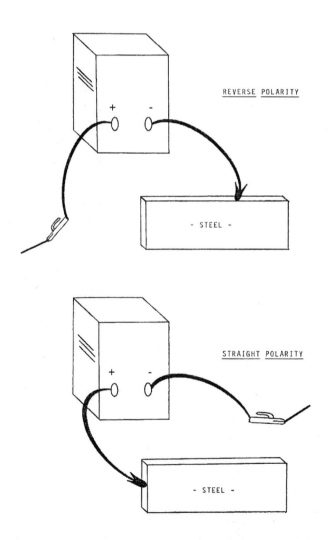

Reverse and straight polarity probable seem backwards but this is the way it works. At first you may have to double check your connections to see which cable is connected to which electric terminal on the welding machine. In time it will become second nature to you.

(B) An Electrode (welding rod)

A welding rod is nothing more than a filler. Its sole purpose is to add more metal to fill the space where the two metals are being joined together. When the arc is established, the electric current is complete (closed) and the welding process is started. The current produces a high heat that melts the metal of the two pieces being joined to form what is referred to as the **Molten Puddle**, fusing the two metals together. This heat also melts the welding rod, blending it into this molten puddle. Since more metal is being added to the joint, the joined area is much stronger. The fusing of the two metals, along with the blending of the metal from the welding rod, is the whole concept behind welding.

Welding has one enemy. If air (oxygen) comes into contact with the molted puddle it will weaken that area of the weld and make it brittle. The reason for this is that the air molecules blend with the metal molecules, thus changing the makeup of the mixture and cools much faster which produces small pin holes throughout the weld, thus making the weld weak and brittle. To prevent this from happening the welding rod is coated with a powdery substance called **Flux**. When the welding rod melts, this flux melts as well. The melted flux flows on top of the molten puddle shielding it from all contact with the atmosphere. As the molten puddle cools so does the flux and all becomes a solid again. The now cooled flux is called **Slag**. All welding is performed with some type of flux or shielding. In some types of welding a gaseous shield is used. This can be a singular gas such as Argon, or a combination of gasses such as Nitrogen and Carbon Dioxide.

There is more to a welding rod than meets the eye. Identification as to the type of welding rod can be a problem. Welding rods used to be color coded. Whatever the color of the powdery substance (or flux coating) on the welding rod told you what type of metal that particular welding rod could be used to weld. This type of identification is obsolete. A numbering system is now used. To explain this numbering system I will use the low-hydrogen welding rod as an example. Each number in the identification code has a purpose.

EXAMPLE: The "7018" Low-Hydrogen Welding Rod

(A) The "70" represents the amount of pressure in pounds per square once needed in order to break the weld. This is known as the **Tensil Strength.** In this example, 70 pounds of pressure per square once is needed to break the weld.

(B) The "1" tells you what position the welding rod can be used for welding. **Position** in welding refers to flat, vertical, or overhead welding. Each position is represented by a number:

"1" = Flat, vertical, or overhead welding may be done with this rod.

"2" = Flat or vertical welding can be done with this rod.

"3" = Flat position welding only by using this rod.

(C) The "8" is the manufacturer's code as to the properties contained within the welding rod.

One thing will hold true for all welding rods. _**You must keep the flux dry!**_ If the flux coating on the welding rod should ever get wet, throw the welding rod away. When the wet flux on the welding rod melts during welding, the water present will evaporate thus blending in with the molten puddle. This will weaken the weld by allowing air to come into contact with the molten puddle.

Welding rods are usually kept dry by storing them in what is called a **Hot Box.** This is a closed container that has a heating element built into it that prevents moisture build-up. You can make your own hot box by using an old, worn out refrigerator. Remove the inner working and install a light but that will stay lit at all times. The light bulb will generate heat thus keeping your welding rods dry until you need them.

(C) The Electrode Holder (Stinger)

The electrode holder's function is to hold the welding rod during welding. The most common term used for the electrode holder is **Stinger**. To simplify matters I will refer to this term whenever I am talking about the electrode holder.

The jaws of the stinger are spring loaded. This is to hold the welding rod tightly in place and prevents the welding rod from slipping during welding. Squeezing the handle opens the jaws; releasing the handle closes the jaws.

Several brand name stingers are on the market and each brand has it advantages and disadvantages. Every welder has a preference as to which brand of stinger they like and use. With time and experience you too will develop a preference.

(D) The Welding Shield

Welding shields basically serve two purposes. One is to protect your eyes, face, and surrounding skin from being burned from the bright light that is present during welding, and from the many sparks that are given off during welding. The second purpose is to reduce the intensity of the light to enable you to see what is actually is taking place while welding the two metals together. This is accomplished by a dark-colored lens that is mounted inside the welding shield (also refer to as a welding helmet).

Welding lenses may be gold in color but the majority of the filter lenses are green in color. Whichever you use, various shades of the color reduces the bright light in various degrees. For example, lighter shades of green filter out less light while the darker shades of green filter out more light. These lenses are labeled numerically with the lowest number being the lightest shade. The middle of the road shade is the #11. Most welders will use a #10 shade when welding outdoors in normal sunlight. Since the surrounding surface space is being well lit by the sun you do not need to filter out as much of the light given off during welding.

On the other hand, most welders will use a #12 shade when welding indoors or when welding outdoors during nighttime. Since the surrounding space is not as well lit as that of being in the sunlight, the light given off during welding is more intense and you need to filter out more of this light. Using a middle of road shade such as the #11 shade will keep you from having to change out the lenses as often.

Welding shields come in different shapes, size, and color depending on the manufacturer of such shield. No matter the shape or size, they all accomplish the same thing. The one major difference in welding shields is the size of the filter lens. One uses the standard size of filter lens measuring 2" x 4 1/4". The other uses a "wide-faced" lens that measures 4 1/2" x 5 1/4". As to which to use is up to you. I personally prefer to use the wide-faced filter lens for it gives me a wide, overall view of the welding area.

BEGINNING TO WELD

Two types of welding rods will be used for all of the examples of the different techniques. This will help you to better understand these examples and reduce the risk of confusion. The welding rod that will be used for the first half of this section will be the low-hydrogen 7018.

There are two reasons for using this type of welding rod. First of all, it is the easiest welding rod to use. Secondly, it is the most popular welding rod used for welding common steel commonly referred to as **Mild Steel.** In the second half of this section I will tell you how to weld with the 6010 welding rod, the second most popular welding rod used for welding common steel.

Each example is written in **Direction Form** because it is easier to follow directions in a step-to-step form than it is to try to follow a paragraph. Nothing is more frustrating than trying to find an answer within a paragraph where you have to sift through a lot of meaningless words. Usually by the time you do find the answer, you have forgotten the question. Hopefully this type of instruction will prevent this from happening.

There are three basic positions for welding steel. Those positions are:

(A) FLAT
(B) OVERHEAD; and
(C) VERTICAL

Objects to be welded can be positioned differently than those mentioned above. Whatever the position your ability to weld in the three basic positions will determine the outcome of these welds.

Where the two pieces of steel, that are to be welded together touch, is called a **Joint.** The four commonly used joints, **Butt Joint, "T" Joint, Lap**

Joint, and *Corner* or *Modified "T" Joint,* are shown in the following example. Study these joints and learn which is which.

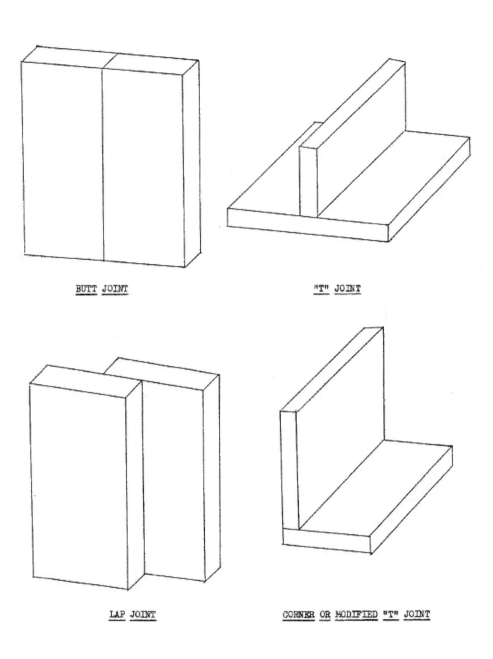

BUTT JOINT

"T" JOINT

LAP JOINT

CORNER OR MODIFIED "T" JOINT

(A) Setting The Welding Machine

In the equipment section of this manual I told you that basically all welding machines work the same. They are designed to produce a wide range of currents better known as *Amps* (amperage). The current produced brings the metal that is being welded, along with the welding rod being used, to their melting points thus forming the *Molten Puddle*. The whole concept behind welding is to bring the welding rod being used to its most efficient melting point that will allow it to flow smoothly and blend in evenly with the molten puddle of the piece being welded. Therefore, setting the welding machine to the correct output is the first step in welding.

All welding machines, with a few exceptions, have a control dial that is set to a predetermined, general range of current. They are set to a range of 10 such as 70, 80, 90, 100, 110, etc. Some dials may even be calibrated for a more wide range of amps such as 60, 80, 100, 120, etc. By setting the welding machine to a predetermined setting, such as "90", means that the output will be 90 amps.

In addition to this control dial, some welding machines have a *Fine Adjustment* dial. This dial is calibrated from "0" to "10" with each mark representing a one or two degree setting (depending on the calibration of the control dial). Its purpose is to fine tune the output from the welding machine to the desired amperage needed to do the welding properly. This will achieve an, "in-between" amperage should it be required.

Example:

(A) If your welding machine is preset to a range of "10" and the desired amperage needed is "90", simply set the control dial to "90" and begin to weld.

(B) If your welding machine is preset to a range of "20" and the desired amperage needed is "90", set the control dial to "80" and adjust the fine adjustment dial. In this example each mark of the fine adjustment dial represents "2" degrees. By setting it to a setting to "5", will give you an additional 10 amps thereby making the overall amp setting to "90".

Do not abuse the fine adjustment dial. If your desired amps needed is "90" set your control dial to "90". Do not set the control dial to "80" and adjust the fine adjustment dial to "10". Granted, this will give you an output of "90" amps but overtime it will prematurely burn out the rheostat of the fine adjustment dial. Remember, the objective here is to achieve the most efficient temperature to achieve the most efficient weld. Only use the fine adjustment dial for an, "in-between" amperage when needed.

FLAT POSITION WELDING

Each step will be given to you in "direction form" followed by, if necessary, an explanation of that step. Please pay close attention to the procedures and techniques given and *never deviate from them*. You need to take this seriously. Any deviation could result in a weak weld that could break resulting in a possible injury or death.

Certain aspects of any trade can only be learned through time and experience while working in that trade. Most call them *"trade secrets"*. Throughout this manual I have passed on a few of these trade secrets. Pay close attention to them, for they will make your job go by a little faster and a little easier, and a little safer.

(A) Using the 1/8" 7018 Low-Hydrogen Welding Rod

(1) **Turn The Welding Machine On.** This may sound ridiculous but you will be surprised as to the number of times you will forget to do so.

(2) **Adjust the control dial, and if possible the fine adjustment dial, to achieve 125 amps.** This should be close to the correct temperature needed for this welding rod. The reason I said "close" is because all welders have a preference as to how many amps they use. Even though 125 amps is recommended for this welding rod does not mean that it won't weld at any other setting. Some welders like to use it a little "hotter" by tweaking up the amps to burn a little hotter thereby penetrating a little deeper into the metal during the welding process. Some welders like the amps a little colder than recommended. Personally, I do not see the reason for using this welding rod at a lower amperage than that recommended.

(3) **Connect your welding cables for REVERSE POLARITY welding.** Also, do not forget to "ground" your work piece.

(4) ***Insert the welding rod into the jaws of the stinger.*** The best way is to have it inserted in a 45 degree angle. Most stingers will have a groove preset just for this. This will help you maintain the molten puddle as you melt your way towards the end of the welding rod by reducing the amount of wrist strain so as to maintain the proper welding rod angle.

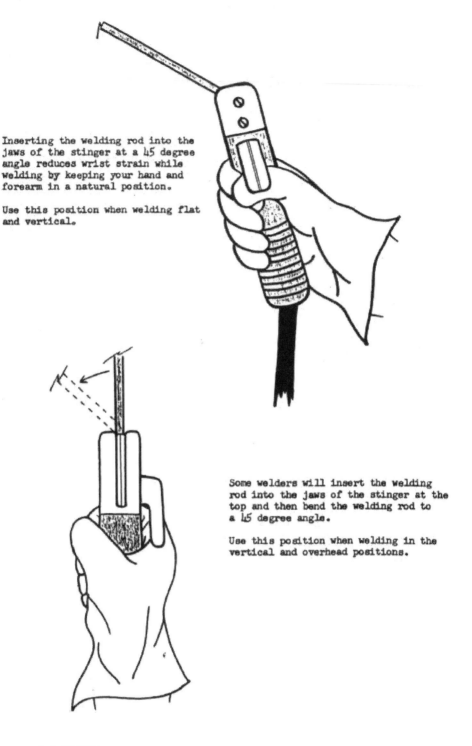

Inserting the welding rod into the jaws of the stinger at a 45 degree angle reduces wrist strain while welding by keeping your hand and forearm in a natural position.

Use this position when welding flat and vertical.

Some welders will insert the welding rod into the jaws of the stinger at the top and then bend the welding rod to a 45 degree angle.

Use this position when welding in the vertical and overhead positions.

TRADE SECRET:

21

Welding rods do bend. Even though you have the welding rod inserted in a 45 degree angle, you may need a little more angle. Instead of having to be a contortionist to be able to reach the place you are welding, simply bend the welding rod before you begin to weld.

You can also achieve this 45 degree angle by inserting the welding rod in the end of the stinger where the welding rod is pointing straight out. Now all you have to do is bend the welding to the angle you desire. Either way it makes your job a little easier and a little more comfortable to perform.

(5) *Strike the arc*. There are two methods of striking the arc.

Tap Method: In this method you *"tap"* the end of the welding rod on the metal at the place you want to begin to weld. This enables you to start welding at your starting point rather than having to search for it once the arc is established.

Match Method: In this method you strike the metal with the tip of the welding rod and drag the tip of the welding rod the same as you would if you were striking a match to make a flame. In this method you will have to search for your starting point to begin welding. One draw back to this method is that it will leave "scratch" marks (which are little bits of metal deposited on the piece being welding) as you search for your starting point. However, when learning to weld, the scratch method is the easier of the two methods when establishing the arc.

Once the arc is established you are welding. This is where the procedures and techniques begin. Welding is done from left to right. There are four things that happen all at once during welding that you *MUST* maintain at all time with each welding rod you use.

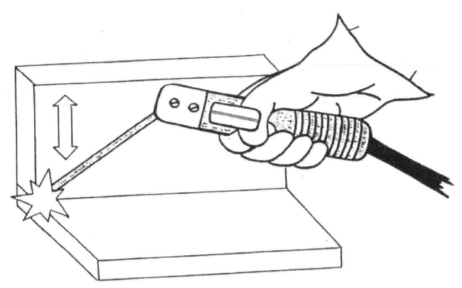

The "TAP METHOD" of striking the arc is done by tapping the tip of the welding rod on the metal at your intended starting point and raising the tip to the correct length of arc without breaking the arc.

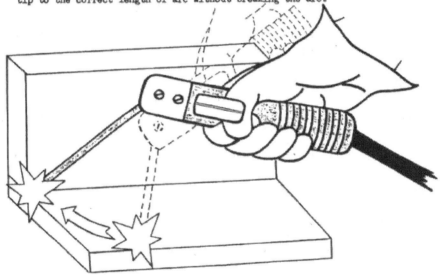

The "MATCH METHOD" of striking the arc is done by striking the tip of the welding rod across the metal like that of a kitchen match and dragging the tip to your intended starting point without breaking the arc.

Length Of Arc: The correct length of an arc is 1/8" from the tip of the welding rod to the metal being welded.   This spacing ensures the most efficient electric current required to simultaneously melt the welding rod and the metal that is being welded.   If you are maintaining the correct length of arc it should sound like bacon frying.   Too much arc and you will hear a blowing sound and penetration into the metal being welded will be lessened. Too little of an arc will make it difficult to establish the arc and cause the welding rod to "stick" (or weld itself) to the metal being welded.

Speed of Travel: This is how fast you move the welding rod from left to right while welding.   You want to keep the molten puddle the same size throughout the entire weld.   Going too fast will lessen the penetration of the weld and the weld will be uneven and skinny in appearance.   Going to slow will cause a build up of metal and the metal will "roll" giving the weld a fat, uneven appearance.   It has been suggested that the proper size of the molten puddle should be that of 1-1/2 times the size of the welding rod being used. Maintaining a slow, even pace will produce just that plus have the maximum penetration into the metal being welded resulting in a strong weld.

Angle of the Welding Rod: The correct angle is achieved by leaning the stinger to the right in the direction you are traveling, at a 45 degree angle. This allows the molten puddle to stay behind the welding rod and does not allow the *flux* to get ahead of the weld.   If flux gets ahead of the weld it can get trapped inside of the weld and you will have a weak spot in that area. You could also lose the arc because the flux will now become a barrier between the welding rod and the metal being welded causing it to break off all electric current.   Imagine if you will a light switch.   As long as the switch is located in the correct position (or angle) the light stays on.   Change that position (or angle) and the light will go off because you have opened (or have blocked off) the circuit.

   If the flux should ever get ahead of the weld you will a "bubbling" effect.   This is your cue to adjust the angle of the welding rod to force the flow of the flux back behind the molten puddle.   When done correctly you will see a nice, even molten puddle.

Size of the Molten Puddle: The correct size of the molten puddle is one and one half (1-1/2) times the size of the welding rod being used. Maintaining the correct size of the molten puddle will result in a good penetration of the weld into the metal and the weld will have a uniform appearance.

All four of the above events will happen at the same time and you will not be aware of them individually. The only one you will actually concentrate on is the size of the molten puddle. By doing so you will automatically be accomplishing the other three.

This is all there is to welding. All that is needed is ***Practice!*** Just how good you get at welding depends upon it. Believe it or not, I just taught you how to weld in the flat position.

No matter what position you are welding, **_ALWAYS_** divide the molten puddle equally on both pieces of metal you are joining together. If the majority of the weld (molten puddle) is on one piece rather than divided equally on both then you have accomplished very little. The two pieces of metal will not be joined securely and the weld will break. This could cause major problems in the quality of work or someone getting hurt.

A completed weld from one end to the other, no matter how may welding rods you used to get to the end, is called a ***PASS***. Sometimes more that one pass is required to strengthen the weld and/or to achieve the size of weld desired. The following is the correct procedure for welding multiple passes, better known as ***tying in the weld.***

First Pass: The first pass of any weld is always referred to as the ***ROOT PASS***. It is placed in such a way that the molten puddle is divided equally between the two pieces of metal being joined together.

Second Pass: This pass is placed a the bottom of the root pass with one third of this molten puddle going onto the metal being welded and two thirds of the molten puddle going onto the root pass.

Third Pass: This pass is placed above the other two passes with one third of the molten puddle going onto the metal being welded and two thirds of the molten puddle going onto the weld. The root pass will now be completely covered and all you will see is the full third pass and a third of the second pass.

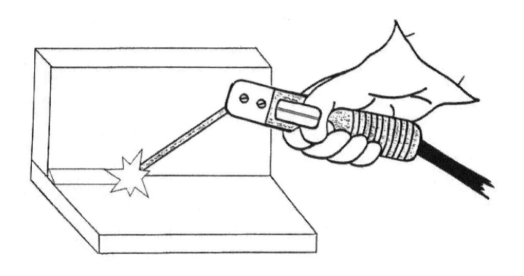

Keep the molten puddle divided evenly on the first (root) pass by having equal halves of the molten puddle on each steel plate.

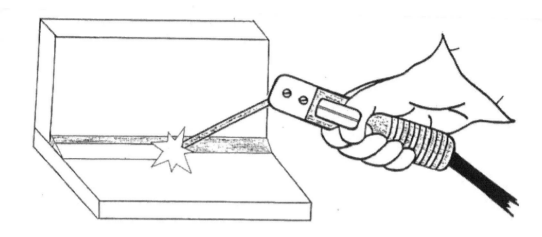

The molten puddle of the second pass covers one third of new steel at the bottom of the root pass, and two thirds on the root pass.

Remember, the second pass is _always_ placed at the bottom of the root pass when welding flat, horizontal, or overhead.

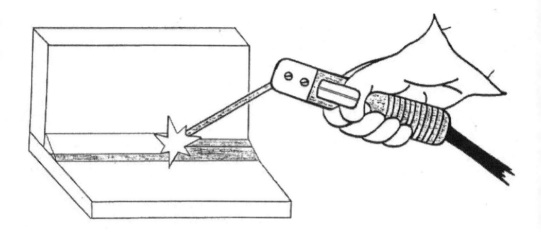

The molten puddle of the third pass covers one third of new steel and two thirds of the second pass.

Upon completion of the third pass the weld is now considered to be reinforced.

Never change the procedure when reinforcing a weld. Doing so will weaken the weld because the second and third pass will not *"tie"* in together as they should.

Never Change This Procedure! Breaking procedure will result in the three passes not being tied together properly. Reversing the placement of the second and third pass will weaken the weld by leaving a weak bond between the second and third pass.

If the weld needs to be reinforced further, or the weld needs to be bigger according to the blueprints, repeat the procedures once more by adding three passes instead of two. Start at the bottom of the weld you have just made and work your way up to the top of weld with the third pass.

The first new pass will cover one third of the root pass and two thirds below it will be on new metal. The second pass will cover one third of root pass and two thirds down on the pass you previously made. The third pass will cover one third up onto new metal and two thirds on the previous second pass.

Each time you reinforce the same weld add another pass. You will follow this procedure on reinforcing a weld:

Root pass – the first pass.
Second pass – the bottom pass.
Third pass – the top pass.

Reinforcing this weld:

First pass – at the bottom.
Second pass – in the middle.
Third pass – at the top.

Adding more passes will reinforce the weld even further. Always start at the bottom and work upwards.

If you need to use more that one welding rod to complete a pass, start the new welding rod where you left off with the previous welding rod overlapping the previous weld by one quarter of an inch. This will eliminate a weak area in the weld. It is <u>required</u> that you first remove the ***Slag*** from the previous weld before beginning to weld with a new welding rod to complete the pass. This will help to prevent slag from being trapped inside the weld, which would leave a weak area in the weld.

Slag is removed from a weld by tapping on it with a hard object. Since slag is brittle this tapping breaks up the slag and allows it to fall off the weld. A special hammer called a ***Chipping Hammer*** (sometimes referred to as a "slag" hammer) is designed just to remove slag. One end of this hammer is wide and flat while the other end is tapered to a point. Since slag ***must*** be removed from each pass before beginning another pass, a chipping hammer makes this task much easier.

OVERHEAD POSITION WELDING

Overhead welding is identical to flat position welding. Many welders have a problem with this position because they get all worked up over the fact that they are welding over their heads. Hence, they fail to follow the four factors necessary to weld. As a result, the weld will be uneven and wavy, or have "droops" of metal hanging down. In welding terms this is known as *Grapes.*

TRADE SECRET: The easiest way to weld overhead is to simply think "*Flat*". As silly as this sounds it really does work. By thinking you are welding "*flat*" will help you in achieving a nice, smooth, uniform weld that has good penetration into both pieces of metal you are joining together.

Sometimes the need will arise to reinforce an overhead weld. The procedure is the same as reinforcing a flat position weld where you start at the bottom of the root pass and work your way up. This would be a good time for you to review the section "*FLAT POSITION WELDING*" of this manual on reinforcing the weld.

As with welding in any position, positioning yourself comfortably before beginning to weld will make the job go by that much more easier. However, a word of caution is in order when welding in the overhead position. Gravity is always pulling downward on the molten puddle as you weld. The slag will have a tendency to drip just like water dripping off the awning of your house after a rain. Watch out for it and position your head, hands, arms, and body in such a way that when it does drip you are not directly underneath it. That hot drop of slag will burn you. That first initial shock of being burned from this hot, dripping slag will teach you rather quickly on how to better position yourself hence forth when welding overhead.

The slag over an overhead weld is one of the ugliest things you will ever see in your welding career. It will look like a roller coaster with its wavy and drooping appearance and you will think you have made a bad weld. Don't let its appearance fool you. The reason it looks this way is because of the gravity effect I told you about. Being hot is will drip rather easily but by cooling so rapidly is what gives it that ugly appearance. Follow the "TRADE SECRET" I told you earlier about thinking "flat" and your weld will be a strong one despite the appearance of the slag covering it.

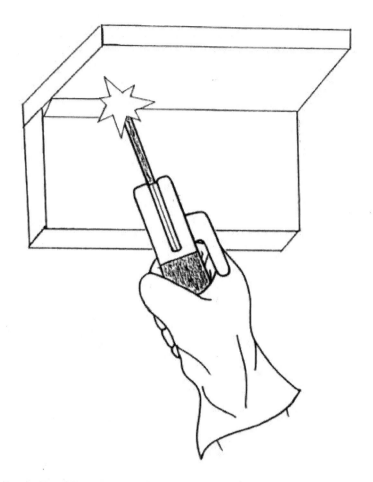

Overhead welding is done the same way as flat position welding. Keep the molten puddle divided evenly on the first (root) pass by having half of the molten puddle on each steel plate.

Remember: Think flat when welding in the overhead position.

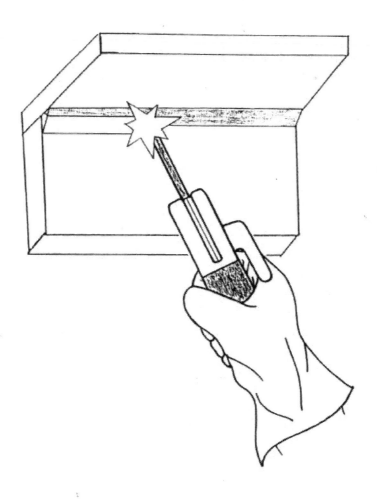

Remember, the second pass is **always** placed at the bottom of the root pass.

The molten puddle of the second pass covers one-third of new steel and two-thirds of the root pass.

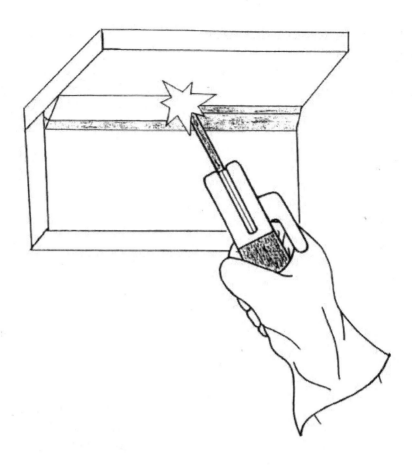

The molten puddle of the third pass covers one-third of new steel and two-thirds of the second pass.

The slag of an overhead weld will look different than that of a flat position weld because gravity is constantly pulling downward on the molten flux. Do not let the appearance of the slag discourage you. If you will remember to "think flat" when welding in the overhead position, your weld will be nice and even.

Overhead welding is very simple and is done exactly as that of flat position welding. Therefore, I need not repeat myself on the procedures of flat position welding. If you will study that procedure described in that section of this manual you will do just fine. Again, *"practice"* is the key word.

VERTICAL POSITION WELDING

Vertical position welding is the hardest to learn and master. As with welding in the overhead position, gravity is constantly pulling the molten puddle downward. It is more evident in vertical position welding because you are moving the molten puddle from side to side while, at the same time, moving upward. If the slag of an overhead weld is one of the ugliest things you will see in your welding career, then the slag covering a vertical position weld will mar you for life for it is the down right <u>most</u> ugly!

The secret to making a good vertical position weld is to just take your time. Concentrate on the four factors necessary for welding we discussed earlier, especially the size of the molten puddle. Remember the gravity effect and position yourself properly. Now, let's learn how to make a vertical position weld.

(A) *Using the 1/8" 7018 Low-Hydrogen Welding Rod*

(1) Set the welding machine for ***Reverse Polarity*** welding.

(2) ***"Ground"*** your work piece.

(3) Set the welding machine about 5 to 50 amps colder than you would if you were welding in the flat position. In other words, about 115 amps. This is to help compensate for gravity pulling downward on the molten puddle.

(4) Position the welding rod in the stinger at a 45-degree angle. Instead of pointing the welding rod at the work piece horizontally, tilt the tip of the welding rod slightly upward.

(5) Strike the arc at the bottom of the place you are going to start to weld. Never strike the arc in the weld area and drag the welding rod down to your intended starting point. Doing so will trap slag behind the weld resulting in a weak area at that point inside the weld. This same slag may also make it difficult in starting and maintaining the arc.

(6) Since welding is done from left to right, establish the molten puddle on the steel piece located on your left before continuing the weld.

(7) Once you have the correct molten puddle size, smoothly move the welding rod straight over to the right to the other piece of metal being welded.

(8) Pause briefly.

(9) Now move the tip of the welding rod smoothly back to the left to the other piece of metal being welded, *"moving slightly upward"* as you move the tip of the welding rod to the left.

(10) Pause briefly.

(11) Repeat steps #7 through #10. By repeating these four steps over and over will produce the vertical position weld.

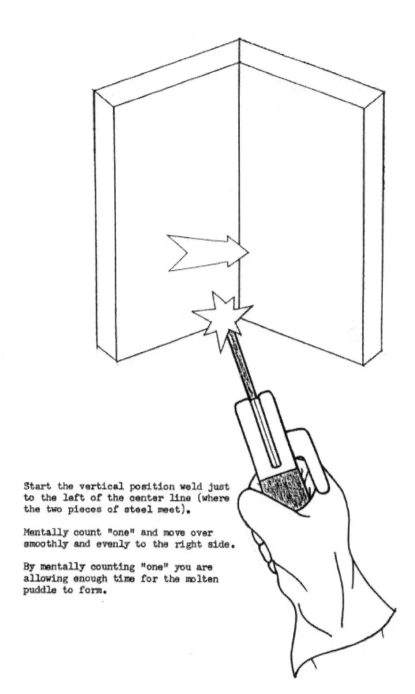

Start the vertical position weld just to the left of the center line (where the two pieces of steel meet).

Mentally count "one" and move over smoothly and evenly to the right side.

By mentally counting "one" you are allowing enough time for the molten puddle to form.

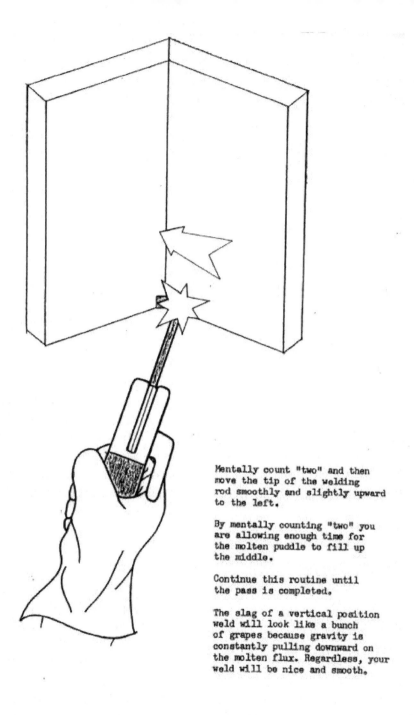

Mentally count "two" and then
move the tip of the welding
rod smoothly and slightly upward
to the left.

By mentally counting "two" you
are allowing enough time for
the molten puddle to fill up
the middle.

Continue this routine until
the pass is completed.

The slag of a vertical position
weld will look like a bunch
of grapes because gravity is
constantly pulling downward on
the molten flux. Regardless, your
weld will be nice and smooth.

38

The trick to vertical welding is to *"pause briefly on each plate"* when you move from side to side. To create this pause mentally count *"one"* while on the left side, smoothly move over to the right side, then mentally count *"two"*. This is how I conditioned myself to pause on each side to allow the molten puddle to regain and to maintain its proper, uniform size.

"Pace yourself when welding vertically!" Going too fast will not allow enough time for the molten puddle to regain its proper size, the middle of the weld will not have enough time to fill itself up, and metal penetration will not be as great. On the other hand, going to slow will allow gravity to take over and pull the molten puddle downward forming a *"droop"* which is referred to as *"grapes"*.

TRADE SECRET: Even though it appears that you are moving over "straight" to the left side, in reality, you are moving slightly upward and over at the same time. This moving over is where a lot of welders foul up. If you will move over smoothly, pause, move back over smoothly, pause, etc. The weld will be a strong, smooth and slick looking weld. Just take it a step at a time and relax!

You now know how to weld in the vertical position. Only by practicing will you ever become good at it. The first few welds you make vertically will be rough looking and will either be rounded in the middle, which is caused by moving over to the other side too slow, or the weld will be conclave (a sunken half moon shape) which is caused by moving over to the other side too fast. With practice you will achieve the ultimate vertical weld, which is smooth and flat.

(B) Reinforcing a Vertical Position Weld

A vertical position weld is reinforced the same way as that of a flat and overhead position weld. The only difference is that instead of going from bottom to top, you go from left to right. Each vertical pass covers the same area of new metal and the previous pass as the ones used in to reinforce a flat or overhead weld. Remember, that coverage is one third of the molten puddle covers new metal while two thirds of the molten puddle covers the previous pass. If you would mentally picture the vertical weld as being a flat weld you will better understand how they are reinforced the same.

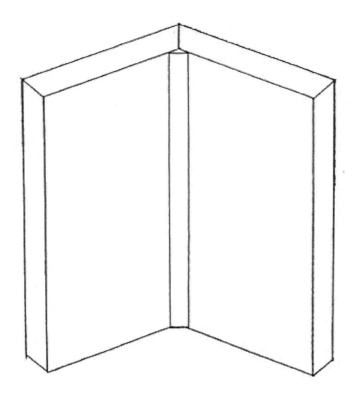

The root pass on a vertical position weld is made by dividing the molten
puddle evenly between the two pieces of steel.

Always start the weld on the left side and move the tip of the welding rod
to the right side. Do not forget to mentally count "one", "two", "one", etc.

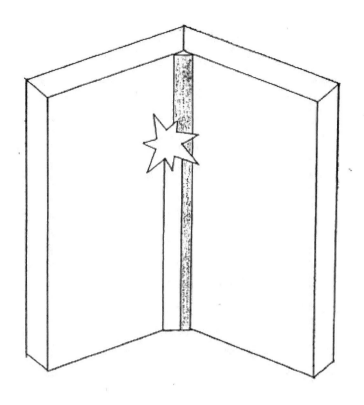

The second pass when reinforcing a vertical position weld is <u>always</u>
started to the left of the root pass.

The molten puddle of the second pass covers one-third of new steel and
two-thirds of the root pass.

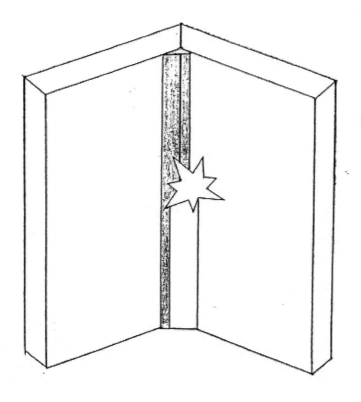

The third pass of a reinforced vertical position weld is <u>always</u> started to the right of the second pass.

The molten puddle of the third pass covers one-third of new steel and two-thirds of the second pass.

(C) Finishing a Vertical Position Weld

Finishing a vertical weld is better known in welding terms as *"Capping Off"* the weld. Because gravity is pulling the molten puddle downward, the top of the vertical weld will be half moon shaped with the "valley" (or middle) of the weld going downward. To help fill this in with weld and make it smooth and uniform in appearance, you do the following:

(1) *Always* complete a vertical weld on the *right hand side* of the weld.

(2) Once you are there, *"break the arc momentarily"* by lifting the tip of the welding rod upward.

(3) Re-establish the arc where you stopped it on the right hand side and *"smoothly move straight over to the left side"*.

(4) Pause briefly and break the arc.

This will be enough to complete the weld and leave it smooth and flat at the top of the weld. You can, if you want, repeat the steps above and move twice from side to side but I do believe that it will be overkill. You be the judge. Your goal is a smooth and uniform capping off of the weld.

You now possess the knowledge of welding in all three basic positions. All that you lack is the experience. *"PRACTICE"* is the only way you can acquire that. Read and re-read this manual until all of the procedures are clear and second nature to you. You will soon develop your own style that is comfortable to you. No matter the style, the procedures *"must be kept and applied"* with <u>NO EXCEPTIONS</u> !

TRADE SECRET: Welders guard their experience and knowledge very closely. Never ignore those who have more experience than yourself. If you give them the impression that you know it all they will do nothing to assist you with your welding. Instead, convey to then that you are interested and willing to listen and learn. They can, and will, teach you things about the art of welding that you would not have thought possible.

THE 6010 *"Wild Steel"* WELDING ROD

This welding rod is used to weld on common steel like that of the 7018 low-hydrogen welding rod. However, it too has its own characteristics and application for use. Many welders use the 6010-welding rod for the root pass, such as when welding pipe joints, for it is a hotter burning welding rod therefore penetration deeper into the metal. This same reason makes it the ideal welding rod to use when welding on rusty metal because it can quickly and easily burn past the rust and corrosion, allowing it to penetrate the good metal which lies beneath.

Another characteristic of the 6010 welding rod is its ability to cool quickly from a molten puddle state and back into a solid state. This makes it the primary welding rod to use when welding on thin steel because the welder is able to form the molten puddle, stop just long enough for the puddle to cool, and re-form the molten puddle once again without melting away the thin steel. Its cooling ability makes it the ideal welding rod to use when filling in a gap between two pieces of metal being welded such as when an improper fit-up or alignment has been made prior to beginning to weld.

The 6010 welding rod is by no means the favorite welding rod used among welders, especially for beginners. One reason is that while in use it throws off a great deal of sparks. These sparks will burn your skin and catch clothing on fire. It is for this reason that protective clothing is strongly recommended. Another reason is the over-all appearance of the finished weld is rough looking rather than nice and smooth as that of the 7018 low-hydrogen welding rod. However, the primary reason for its lack of popularity is mastering the technique for welding with the 6010-welding rod.

Whereas the procedure for welding will always remain the same, the technique for welding depends upon the type of welding rod being used. For example, the 7018 low hydrogen welding rod is considered to be a *"drag"* type of welding rod because the proper technique for using it is to drag the tip of the welding rod smoothly and uniformly from left to right, keeping the molten puddle a constant size throughout the entire welding process.

The 6010 welding rod is considered as a *"whipping"* type of welding rod because its technique during use calls for a whipping action back and forth while moving from left to right in order to form and keep the molten puddle a constant size throughout the entire welding process.

Since this section concentrates on the 6010-welding rod, the first step is to determine the correct temperature setting for the welding machine. One quick way to remember the temperature setting for the welding machine for this type of welding rod is to set the welding machine as if you are going to weld with a 7018 low hydrogen welding rod *"ONE SIZE SMALLER"* than the 6010 welding rod you plan to use. In other words, if you are welding with a 1/8" 6010 welding rod, set the temperature on the welding machine as if you were going to be welding with a 3/32" 7018 low-hydrogen welding rod. You may have to move the fine adjustment dial to dial in on the desired temperature you want to use. Bear in mind that has their own preference as to how "hot" or how "cold" they burn each type of welding rod. One day you too will develop your own preference.

As I stated earlier in this manual, the whole concept behind welding is to bring the welding rod being used to its most efficient melting point that will allow it to flow smoothly and blend in evenly with the molten puddle of the piece being welded. This holds true for every type of welding rod on the market. The temperature range needed to produce the most effective melting point varies among the different welding rods because each welding rod requires its own heat range. Every welding supply store has a chart that list this information for every type of welding rod currently being used in the trade.

(A) Using the 1/8" 6010 Welding Rod

(1)   Set the welding machine for **REVERSE POLARITY** welding.

(2)   Determine the set the temperature setting on the welding machine like that mentioned in the previous section.

(3)   **GROUND** the piece you are going to weld.

(4)   Welding from left to right, strike the arc using either the *tap method* or the *match method.*

(5)   Keep the welding tip at your starting point just long enough for the molten puddle to round out and form to the correct size.

(Remember: the correct size of the molten puddle is one and one half times the size of the welding rod being use.)

(6)   Once the molten puddle has formed to the correct size, back the tip of the welding rod out of the molten puddle by moving it straight to the right about ½".

(7)   **_Do Not Break The Arc_** - just hesitate long enough to mentally count **_"one"_**. This hesitation allows the molten puddle you just formed to cool back into a solid state.

(8)   Now move the welding rod tip back to the left onto the molten puddle you have just let cool down and for another molten puddle to the correct size again. *Let this new molten puddle cover half of the previous puddle and the other half of this new molten puddle to cover new steel.*

(Refer to the illustration to better understand the to see how it is to look.)

(9)   Repeat this *"in and out"* movement of the welding rod tip until you have reached your stopping point. The pass is now complete.

The slag covering a weld made by a 6010 welding rod is different looking from the slag covering a weld made by a low hydrogen welding rod. Instead of *"pecking"* the slag off with a chipping hammer like you would on a low hydrogen weld, simply *"scrape"* the tip if the chipping hammer across the entire weld and the slag will come off easily. Wire brush the weld to remove any excess slag.

You have now made a **_FLAT POSITION WELD_** using the 6010 welding rod. The *"in and out"* movement of the welding rod tip is referred to as **_"whipping the rod"_** and will require a great deal of practice to master. If done properly, no matter what position you are welding (flat, overhead, or vertical), the completed pass will look like a roll of dimes stacked with each dime laid half way over the previous dime.

Form and place each molten puddle
as shown in this sectional close up.

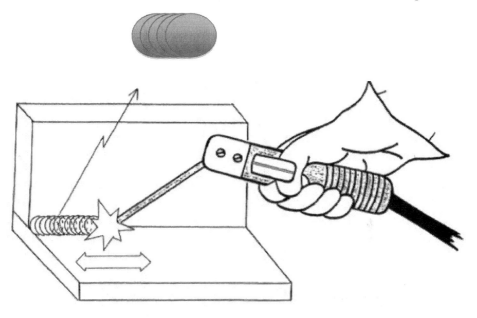

Strike the arc and hold the welding tip in place just
long enough for the molten puddle to round out and
form.

Move the welding rod tip slightly to the right and
hesitate just long enough for the original molten
puddle to cool.

Move the welding rod tip back to the left and form
another molten puddle with half of the molten
puddle on the previous puddle and half on new
steel.

Repeat until the pass is completed.

OVERHEAD POSITION WELD *(Using the 6010 Welding Rod)*

Remember what you have learned about *"whipping the rod"*. Just like over overhead position welding with the low hydrogen welding rod, think **"Flat"** when welding overhead with the 6010 welding rod. Keep your temperature setting on the welding machine the same as when welding in the flat position.

All welding requires protective clothing especially when welding with the 6010 welding rod. This is especially true when welding overhead with the 6010-welding rod. The amount of sparks given off during welding will shower down upon you as you weld overhead. Remember to position yourself in such a way that will allow you to avoid dripping slag and the welding sparks. Welding is a lot more fun when you are not getting burned!

VERTICAL POSITION WELDING *(Using the 6010 Welding Rod)*

(1) Turn the temperature setting on the welding machine down about 10 amps. This is to compensate for the gravity effect mentioned in the first half of this manual.

(2) Strike the arc at the bottom of the piece to be weld.

(3) Hold the welding rod tip at your starting point just long enough for the molten puddle to form to the correct size.

(4) **"Without breaking the arc"** move the tip of the welding rod upward about ½" and hesitate just long enough to mentally count **"one"**. This will allow the molten puddle you have just made to cool back into a solid state.

(5) Back down onto the molten puddle you have just let cool down and stay there long enough for a new molten puddle to form. Let this new molten puddle cover half of the previous one and the other half covering new steel.

(6) Repeat this us and down movement of the welding rod tip until you have reached your stopping point. You now have completed a vertical position weld.

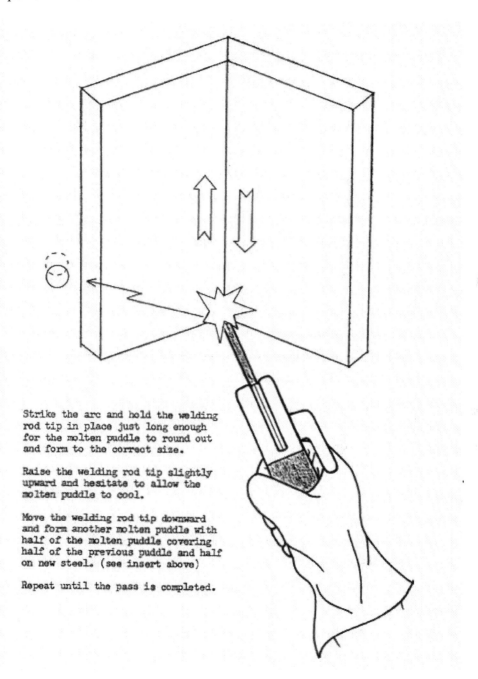

Strike the arc and hold the welding rod tip in place just long enough for the molten puddle to round out and form to the correct size.

Raise the welding rod tip slightly upward and hesitate to allow the molten puddle to cool.

Move the welding rod tip downward and form another molten puddle with half of the molten puddle covering half of the previous puddle and half on new steel. (see insert above)

Repeat until the pass is completed.

When you have reached your stopping point at the top of the pass you will not have as much metal to fill up as you did when welding vertically with a low hydrogen welding rod. To *"cap off"* the vertical weld make with a 6010 welding rod, just keep forming the molten puddle over and over again at the same place. Two or three times doing this should be enough to complete the pass and leave a nice, even line at the top of the pass.

REINFORCING THE WELD IN ALL THREE POSITIONS
(*Using the 6010 Welding Rod*)

No matter what welding rod you use, whether it be the low hydrogen, the 6010 welding rod, stainless steel welding rod, etc, the procedure for reinforcing a flat, overhead, or vertical position weld remains the same. You always go from bottom to top for all flat and overhead position welds. You go from left to right on all vertical position welds.

NEVER CHANGE THIS PROCEDURE IN ANY WAY !

THE *"EXPERIENCE"* CORNER

This is where you learn some well known facts about welding the easy way rather than having to learn them through *"trial and error"*. To be honest, most of these I learned the hard way. However, early in my welding career I had enough sense to realize that I did not *"know it all"* and started paying close attention to what the *"old timers"* were saying and it worked. I actually learned a thing or two about this rewarding trade.

This random list of some little, well known facts will save you a lot of time and trouble. Take the time to read them and, as time goes on, you too will be able to add a few *"known facts"* to this list.

(1)   A weld is stronger than the metal itself because the molecules are packed closer together. Therefore, the metal should break first instead of the weld breaking.

(2)   You can put a stronger metal (weld) on top of a weaker one but never vice-versa. For example, you can weld stainless steel welding rods on regular steel and it will hold. On the other hand, you cannot weld a low-hydrogen welding rod onto stainless steel for it will not bond. The properties within the two metals are different which could result in a broken weld.

(3)   Welds have a lot of *"pulling power"*. The steel will pull into the weld every time. Keep this in mind whenever you *"tack weld"*. If you want the steel to move in a certain direction, such as if the steel is leaning a little more to one side, tack weld it on the opposite side and it will draw the steel towards it. For example, if the steel is leaning to the left and it needs to be moved a little to the right, tack weld it on the right hand side and let the weld pull the metal towards itself, moving the steel to the right.

(4)   Since welds do have a lot of pulling power, welding a long pass continually could cause the steel to warp into a *"bow"* shape or, for example, look like a banana. To avoid this from happening, do what is referred to as **"Back Stepping".** It is done by staggering your welds rather than continuing on with your welding in a straight line.

For example, start at your starting point and weld until that welding rod is finished. Start the next welding rod somewhere else on the piece being welded which do not connect to the previous weld. Continue with this random placement of the weld until you eventually will have all the welds connected into one, long pass.

What you have accomplished by doing this is controlling how much pulling power the weld will have by limiting the distance it can pull. Eventually you will have to tie in to one of your previous welds. Do so at random and continue this style until the entire weld is complete. Your end result will be two pieces of steel welded together with very little distortion in its shape.

(5)   If you have a gap between two pieces of metal you can fill up that gap by turning your heat range cooler than you normally would weld. Add a little weld to one side of this gap and then switch and add a little weld to the other side. Continue this way until the gap is filled. Now you can continue on with your welding as you normally would.

(6)   When welding on anything that has pressure in it, such as a pipe, the weld (or molten puddle) will *"walk"* or be pulled in the direction the pressure in the pipe is traveling. If the pressure is great enough and the metal is hot enough due to being welded upon, the pressure will *"blow"* or break through the pipe directly at the welder. This could be deadly for the welder if the pressure and pressure temperature is great enough. Therefore, never weld on anything that has pressure on or in it.

Just a quick note: This *"walking"* of the weld is a dead give away that the pipe, or whatever you are welding on, has pressure on or in it. Best thing to do is to stop welding immediately and release the pressure.

(7)   Never take anything for granted or someone's word as always being true. *Always check things out for yourself!* People, my friend, will get you killed because they either take it for granted that you already know the circumstances, or they simply forget to tell you the circumstances. From experience, and a lot of pain, I have found this to be true.

(8)   While we are on scary subjects, here is another one that is very important to remember. Never weld on anything such as tanks, steel drums, etc., without first finding out what they once, or now have, stored inside them. If there are fumes present inside they could be flammable. If you strike an arc, which will now provide a heat source, you could very well have an explosion happening in the very near future. When in doubt, *TURN THE WELDING MACHINE OFF!*

(9)   Never weld in the rain. Never allow your welding gloves to become wet when welding. Doing so will be a *"shocking"* experience.

(10)   A welding rod will bend. I have seen a lot of welders look like contortionists because they will not bend a welding rod while it is in the stinger in order to weld in a tight area or hard to get to place. Bending the welding rod to the angle you need before you weld will save you a lot of time and discomfort.

(11)   If you are going to weld, take the time to knock the slag off the finished weld. This will not only make your work more appealing but will enable you to inspect the weld. Welding is made up by may habits. Please make this a good one to have.

(12)   Do not be taken in by all of those *"man made"* tools such as sky - hooks, metal stretchers, etc. No such tools exist. They are made up to make the beginner look like a fool to his boss and co-workers. Try not to fall for them.

These are just a few of the many tips on welding that will make your job that much easier. The biggest tip of all is this:

(13)   ***Never let anyone know just how much you do know!*** The welder who brags about his welding, or how much he knows about welding, is the type of welder you need to put a lot of distance away from you. He, or she, is the one who will probably get you injured. The more someone talks about his or her welding and welding experience the less I trust them. Please take this next statement to heart. If you want to impress someone about your welding, do so with your work and not your words.

SUMMARY

This is how you weld. Nothing is very hard about it and the only way to get good at welding is to just do it. With each welding rod used you will be that much better. No book or manual can make you a welder. All they can do is give you guidelines to go by and procedures to follow. Only by putting what they provide you to use, along with practice and time, can you master this art and become a craftsman.

There are many kinds of welding. You have just learned about *"arc" welding"* or what some people refer to as **"stick welding".** Remember this. No matter what specialty welding you may do, maintaining the arc is the key to welding.

Two of the most popular *"specialty-welding"* are **MIG** (Metal Inert Gas) and **TIG** (Tungsten Inert Gas) welding. In MIG welding a gas is used, usually carbon dioxide or a combination of it with other gasses, instead of a flux material to shield air from getting into the molten puddle. Instead of using a welding rod, a continuous wire feed fed from a spool is used. This requires a special type of stinger and other attachments.

I have to mention one thing about MIG welding. Where most MIG welding is achieved using a gas cloud to shield the molten puddle, there is a special MIG wire that produces a flux coating that covers the molten puddle. This special wire is called **"Flux Core"** and is a hollow wire that is filled with a flux material. When the wire melts the flux is released and the heat produced during welding melts the flux and it flow on top of the molten puddle just as the flux does on a welding rod.

In TIG welding, a special stinger us used that has a tip made of tungsten inserted in it. Again, a gas is used instead of a flux material to shield the molten puddle from air. This is done very much the same way as soldering where you use a separate rod material held in one hand while the other hand controls the stinger. By use of an electric arc, the stinger heats and melts the metal creating a molten puddle. The rod held in the other hand is then inserted and melts in a *"dripping"* fashion into the molten puddle. The rod itself is the filler. This type of welding takes a great deal of practice and is usually used when welding very thin metal or other special metals such as aluminum. Because TIG welding is somewhat more difficult those who do it are usually paid more money for their expertise. Again, practice is the only way to achieve this level of experience.

My final comment to you is this. No matter which type of welding you do, do it **_safely_**! I cannot emphasize this enough. Nothing is worth doing at the risk of sacrificing your safety and that of others. Check and re-check your surroundings before starting to weld. One day you will feel as strong about this as I do.

Have fun welding! It can really be rewarding. The key to the art of welding is ***Practice, Practice, Practice and more Practice!*** I do hope that one day you too will feel the pride of being so well skilled in this remarkable trade. Learn and grow with welding. Have fun but most of all . . . ***Be Safe!***

GLOSSARY OF WELDING TERMS

AMPS: The strength of a current of electricity expressed in amperes. All welding is done in amps.

ARC: A sustained luminous discharge of electricity across a gap in a circuit or between electrodes.

BLOW OUT: While welding, the metal reaches its melting point and the weld goes completely through the metal. In other words, you have burned a hole through the steel.

CHIPPING HAMMER: A special hammer that is pointed on one or both ends that is used to remove slag from a weld. This hammer may also be pointed on one end and flat on the other end.

DINGLE BERRIES: The slang term used for describing weld splatter.

DOWNHILL: A vertical weld made by starting the weld at the top of the metal and welding downward. This type of weld has very little penetration into the steel and is a considerable weak weld and is never recommended.

FLUX: The coating on a welding electrode and / or substance used to promote fusion especially on metals or minerals.

GRAPES: The slang term to describe that part of a weld where the molten puddle ran or dripped and is hanging from the weld.

GROUND: A conducting body used as a common return for an electric current.

HEAT: The amount of amperage (amps) used for welding.

LOW-HYDROGEN: A term used to describe a welding electrode of the "70" series.

MATCH *METHOD*: A method of establishing the arc by "dragging" the welding electrode tip across the metal to the intended starting point.

MILD *STEEL*: A term used to describe the welding electrodes of the "60" series. This term can also be used as another name for common steel.

PASS: Once complete weld from beginning to end no matter how many welding electrodes were used.

REVERSE *POLARITY*: The electric current passes from the "ground" through the object being welded and then returns to the welding machine through the electrode holder.

SCRATCH *MARKS*: The mark left on metal by dragging the electrode tip across the metal such as when establishing the arc via the "match method". It is characterized by a series of minute weld spots deposited in a line.

SLAG: The residue left on top of a weld as a result of burned flux.

SPLATTER: Small metal particles thrown off during welding that usually sticks to the metal that is being welded.

STINGER: The slang term used to describe the electrode holder.

STRAIGHT *POLARITY*: The electric current passes from the electrode holder through the object being welded and returns to the welding machine through the "ground" cable.

STRIKING *THE* *ARC*: The term used to describe the start of the welding process when the electric current is complete and the arc is established.

STRINGER: The slang term used to describe one competed weld pass.

TACK *WELD*: A small weld generally used to hold two pieces of metal together.

TAP METHOD: A method of establishing the arc by "tapping" the tip of the welding electrode on the metal at the intended starting point.

TENSIL STRENGTH: The greatest longitudinal stress (as pounds per square inch) a substance can bear without tearing apart.

UPHILL: A vertical weld that is made by starting the weld at the bottom of the metal and traveling upward.

WELDING PROCEDURE: A series of steps followed in a definite order to produce a certain type of weld on a certain type of metal.

WILD STEEL: The slang term used to describe welding electrodes of the "60" series mainly the 6010 welding rod.

Made in the USA
San Bernardino, CA
14 September 2016